SYNONYMS FOR SILENCE

SYNONYMS FOR SILENCE

poems

A. Molotkov

ACRE

CINCINNATI 2019

Acre Books is made possible by the support of the Robert and Adele Schiff Foundation.

Printed in the United States of America
First Printing

Library of Congress Cataloging-in-Publication Data
Names: Molotkov, A., (Anatoly), author.
Title: Synonyms for silence : poems / A. Molotkov.
Description: Cincinnati : Acre Books, 2019.
Identifiers: LCCN 2019003780 (print) | LCCN 2019010190 (ebook) | ISBN
    978-1-946724-15-1 (ebook) | ISBN 978-1-946724-14-4 (paperback)
Subjects: | BISAC: POETRY / American / General.
Classification: LCC PS3613.O49 (ebook) | LCC PS3613.O49 A6 2019 (print) |
    DDC 811/.6—dc23
LC record available at https://lccn.loc.gov/2019003780

Designed by Barbara Neely Bourgoyne
Cover art: Photograph by Clem Onojeghuo on unsplash.com

The press is based at the University of Cincinnati, Department of English and Compara-
tive Literature, McMicken Hall, Room 248, PO Box 210069, Cincinnati, OH 45221-0069.

Acre Books books may be purchased at a discount for educational use. For information
please email business@acre-books.com.

I am learning
the descensions and ascensions of
silence.

—DAN PAGIS

CONTENTS

OXYGEN

SYNONYMS FOR SILENCE

BROKEN BORDERS

a river
crosses a border
without a visa

I am tired
yet my mind jumps out of bed
and sings

listen, Butterfly!

be careful
take good care of your wings
the world has rough edges
dangerous borders
tall buildings
burning airplanes

A LOVE LETTER TO CHEMISTRY

I believe in rust, its malignant vitality, its firm
love for every surface that will love it back. I admire

the way snowflakes

remember last melting. Trees care little for warmth if
it's not a fire. I wish I could be that confident. I wish

I grew on a hill. I would

give anything to be pure water or
pure ash. I have

no shot at heroism. Oxygen

plays different games with me. My lungs
rust differently. I'm in love with their graying

branches. I admire the way

nothing I say makes the snow melt. I believe
in succumbing to nature. Trees

hear better with their eyes

closed.

CARBON

This cell belongs to a brain, and it is my brain, the brain of the me who is writing; and the cell in question, and within it the atom in question, is in charge of my writing, in a gigantic minuscule game which nobody has yet described.

—PRIMO LEVI

KEY

This side
of the river's falling,

the gaping
mouth of light, its golden

whisper. This must be

how we open and are
replaced. A red

barn, a white
horse.

ON FIRE, LOVE, KILLING, AND OTHER ITEMS

You say, *Fire doesn't matter,*
it just dances the periphery like lost thoughts.
I ask if distance grows on trees,
if loneliness is what leaves whisper.

You say, *Let the forest guide you home.*
When a branch breaks, many leaves are released.

I know for a fact: not all green things
speak the same language. I've tried this before.
If I see you again, I'll be old, my heart lost
to the wind like the leaves. To wood, fire matters.
If you listen to a tree, become its center,
you will learn to love what kills you.

UNFINALITY

The dead enter, lazy handfuls of light through the fence. We've been making room for them to correct us. Between summer and silence, white flowers and your body on the grass. In the end, the amputation of self is a simple act, a gesture of acceptance. Our endless conversations, and life itself, a dream before being dreamed. If you disagree, perhaps the labor of forgetting is light on your shoulders. In the better tomorrow, we will be laughed at. Let them laugh. Let them pick your body from the grass, take it carefully on its journey. We are here for merriment and blood and forgiveness. The dead watch us, smiling. Speeding past our mistakes has long been our tactic. In the end, what do we have to be lost by? We speak through our work: sheltering the storm, naming the rainbows, whispering clouds to sleep.

AGRICULTURAL ADVICE

. . . a cow and I once studied each other over a fence
while the car ticked and cooled behind me.
—ANNIE LIGHTHART

In the distance, a cow emits its one-
note comment on sunlight
and the lovely grass. When
I was a child, years
stretched into unremembered
nothing. Now,
existence demands a more
detailed commitment.

*

The cow sleeps standing. I used
to, when I was a soldier. In some way,
I still am, but this thought may be too
complicated for this context.

*

What is the context?
Who am I to ask?

*

The difference between us is love
and fear. So is
the similarity. The cow loves
the field, and this love is
mutual. The grass loves

the cow's many stomachs, not
knowing which stomach is which,
without a memory of its place
in the dirt.
I know even less, and still
I wake to every
day without
despair.

*

And fear? We almost forgot
about the bees in
the grass, obsessed
with their queen and their
flowers. They sing
their one-
note song, they die
their one-
sting death. And who's
to say one
note is not
a symphony.

*

What is my commitment?
Am I the cow in this context?
I'll chew on this
grass, just
in case.

CORRECTION

as I sing to you   all ships will arrive on schedule   in correct ports

as I sing to you   there will be no mistakes

while I sing   the universe   will run as planned

all of it

with its suns   its black holes   its people   its dragons   its dragonflies

LATE TO THE WORLD

Snowflakes land on my eyelashes
as I step into the yard
to mow the lawn.

A ripe cherry
falls frozen
into my hand.

Icicles on the roof
melt over blooming flowers.

Every question I ask
is answered in another life.

Every person I love
dies
before I can tell them about it.

UNCHRONOLOGY

Ice is on my side when it comes
to things that matter,

a convincing demonstration

of temporality. Ice in a glass is
a step to the next level, or a slow

slide. Confusion reigns. The tree

forms knots, not rings. Years
shrink. Thoughts grow instead

of branches. Ice in a freezer is
still fragile: many perils affect

electricity, and the fridge is about

to break, if not today, then next
year, next life. Ice, a symbol for

the cold world that crushes us—

and we must agree that being crushed is
our goal after all. Ask the iceberg

about temporality. Interrogate

the polar bear, the drowning skater. The tree
sheds its time. Its branches droop.

Its trunk is thinner and

thinner each
year.

A BRIGHT PILE OF REASONS

Perhaps you wake with a start, a stranger, a headache,
an earthquake, an enemy. Perhaps your house

is on fire, or just your mind. You don't

remember how you got here. A burned-out
lightbulb on a wire. A dusty room. It's not

enough to be alive; our species

demands a story, a reason
behind a pile of bones. And our own

miniature worlds inside our skulls, what

rules do they follow? Is the sun I see
the same sun you find in your sky? And if

my brain dwelled in your head, would your

headache be different? These imprecise
identities we live in, polish as time

fades us. A light

bulb on
a wire. A dark

room.

SINCE ALL YOUR FRIENDS

decided to sleep inside your body, you've had the plumbing to consider.
The picky ones expect their own rooms, to engage in odd private acts.
These demands perplex the surgeon as she folds your dermis
and moves around your fat layers, forming a judgment about their abundance.
What scares you isn't sharing yourself—you are used to it—
it's all the air your friends will exhale. It's how much air
you've shared already. You might let them down by not breathing enough.
You might suffocate your friends trapped inside you.
Will you cry when the coroner extracts them from your body,
or did you cry long ago, knowing everything, always hurting in advance?

VIOLIN LESSON

An old man is like a violin:
he remembers the tree
he was made of. The tree
remembers being a man. If we cross

the river, will the water
remember us? If the river's
memory had to track each
rivulet, it would burst

into an ocean. The old man
moves in slow motion
because his feet
remember the truth:

nothing ends, not if you are
part of the ending. The river
remembers the bridge.
Remembering our crossing

is the ocean's job.
The old man is
the ocean. The river,
a violin.

Let's play it.

INNER ISLANDS

Archipelagoes of meanings we build around us, making
        things less simple than they want to be: islands of
                interpretations growing spontaneously out of deep waters,

each with its own port, a tower, the tower's shadow, and many
        frozen faces like in that picture from the days when we believed
                we could last—but now water seeps carefully through our bones.

*

I invented an island for you and you called it Star.

*

Even burned, that picture you took lingers in my memory—
        just because you drowned, you are no less
                true—but now that so many years foam at my door, I know

distance is how time settles into true
        pictures, and still the tower supports the sky,
                our lungs filled with autumn.

*

Red letters where the sea meets its end.

*

You grow an island inside you, then you
        grow more—once started, few things
                want to end; waves are not tired of their

endless exercise, and the tower, not tired
        of supervising; the island grows
                trees, a beach, an inn, a few houses, a cemetery.

*

We are too distant to be helped.

*

Perhaps the island is just a symbol for
        a continent, the tower a stand-in for a taller
                tower, like being in a boat filling with water is

a substitute for a future—
        the way the water fills everything
                with meaning, empties everything of meaning.

*

The heart is not tired of its endless exercise.

*

In the picture, you look
        somewhere past the lens, and I imagine
                you including all that land and all

that sky, its every cloud, as if just that
        configuration of vapor could make
                a lasting difference, as if by being

remembered, one could
        stay; after all, you invented
                an island for me and called it Scar.

*

We seep carefully through our bodies, linger.

*

Archipelagoes grow, the tower crumbles more each
        century—we can't hold it up as we lay our lazy bones
                to rest; the ocean turns into the next, written in red letters—what

matters is what matters, not what's
        true, and I call your life *undrowning*: after
                all, endings make us real, turn us into us.

TO THE FIRM WORLD

I respect concrete, its allegiance to its own
principles, its firm stance, its victory over living
things. In love,

concrete is stronger than gravel or sand. I am
suspicious of strength. I prefer
mystery to certainty in thought but not love, wind,

not smoke, under my wings. Roads
with sad signs. Graves. Buildings. When the day
ends, it has not ended for me. And if life

ends against concrete, who
am I to say?

BATTLEFIELD

You danced the distance,
and it broke you. Or should I

say you broke under it?
You had to cool your fear

of solitude. You walked into a snow-
covered field, you kept walking

until your toes froze. You didn't know
how to cross another way. I waited

at the coffee shop. The street kept running,
unable to escape itself, but you

changed it by not being here. Your blue
eyes focused on an impossible distance,

you forged ahead. You walked
until your thoughts froze. You must

have had a grand time. A snow-
covered smile froze to your face.

I would have walked with you, but I
wasn't there.

THE TILT

The difference between a road and a lake. Between a snake and a traveler headed to sea. A strange kind of distance. A murdered son says to a murdered parent, *Bring me back.* But I died long before you. Your blood can't find my hands. The glow of new victories over the gray horizon leads us on to more slaughter. The snake asks the traveler, *Whose side are you on? You are tilted,* the hills tell the sky. *Whose side is this tree on?* you ask. *And the river?* A dead worm asks the bird, *Why me?* And the bird cleans its feathers without an answer. The cat stills for a leap. The difference between a snake and open fire is whose side you're on. You are tilted, like the rest of the grass. Like the traveler's body at sea.

OPENED

I watch a snowflake
shape its notion of water
into symmetry.

My eyes open me.

I'm a mandala built
to be
erased,
a snowflake, a former crystal,

now
a waterdrop,

now

a memory.

MOON IN THE RIVER

The sun is out

of breath from its decline.
Even the heart goes

to seed and scatters.

Best bridges burn fast.
The sky is a horse, a rusty key

that opens nothing. If I had time, I would

count the dust. Autumn hangs
over winter, a lush

curtain keeping the truth out.

The sun longs for night. Even the past is
not ours. Memory goes

to seed.

Best winds blow
by before we notice.

I'm nowhere. The sky is locked, too

far to be true. Only one direction
exists, but we are

in no rush. Even the heart stops.

Best rivers run out.
If I had only one

horse, I would not

name it.

BRIDGE BUILDING

We are here to scare and be
scared. We trust in skin and what's
on either side, the unseen
and the aging. Skin holds
me in, a shape and a prisoner.

*

Skin's eyes are also mine; this
scar on my wrist, an unfinished
exit. I don't believe
in survival. And the blade sings, reflects
light, commands meaning.

*

I'm not complaining, my blood
inside me. Skin stands,
a tower with small
windows, a method of being
inside and out at the same time.

*

I live between
skin and the tighter
skin I remember. Shall I
rethink this life, fading,
the deepest tattoo?

*

We need a sharper cut, a taller
tower. We need the scar
to survive the scar. A narrow
bridge gleams over each cut. Turn me
inside out to start.

PONTIST'S DREAM

In memory of Gene Mandel,
March 5, 1920–June 5, 2010

a painting does not solve hunger
it just breathes

a symphony does not cure illness
it simply floats

a poem
is not even there

may all the impractical things
burst into being
for the senseless sake of beauty

may we spend our lives
building a bridge
without the excuse
of a river

DRIVING LESSON

We drive through the intense sun,
and the fields listen. The dead
wave, but we don't
see them in the glow
of our optimism. The ending
is already written, but we
have not been told. The dead
hear us. They are in no rush
to speak. They chew
on blades of grass. They lean
on the horizon, trying
to make more room
on this side. And the rain
is different, more engaged in
its touch, as if we had
already arrived. The car
rushes through
the setting light. Our past
recedes behind us like someone
else's mistake. The rusty
engine runs in simple
engine harmony.
And the dead don't
mind that we drag our lives
along wherever we go,
that we are lost so deep
in ourselves
we need a car
to get out.

IRON

A few months before, the racial laws against the Jews had been proclaimed, and I too was becoming a loner. My Christian classmates were civil people; none of them, nor any of the teachers, had directed at me a hostile word or gesture, but I could feel them withdraw and, following an ancient pattern, I withdrew as well: every look exchanged between me and them was accompanied by a minuscule but perceptible flash of mistrust and suspicion. What do you think of me? What am I for you?

—PRIMO LEVI

VICTORY

A village square, a bombed-out
well. Are you thirsty? Will you remember
our names? A still dog chained
to the gate. Do you think it's asleep?

METAL, DECIPHERED

Bombs fall, gray petals that crack
the body's puzzle. We know how it bends

to metal's will, how it forgets

the meaning it carries, when broken. Some
say the meaning goes elsewhere. I

want to see it. Burned eyes are petals

from a black rose, even in our dreams. You
dream too, we've seen your eyes

rush under lids at the checkpoint

of subconscious, burn through stolen scenes, what
others felt when bombs inquired. You know

the body's unanswered question.

If petals are made of ash, what can we tell
about the flower, its smell, its proud

posture, it's short-lived optimism? Some

say the meaning is made after. I
want to see it.

UNHISTORY

Light in big gulps, and down the river, the certainty of great rocks. Many, like I, are going down—and the soundtrack in tomorrow's forgotten languages while today's victims are selected. In the gaps below rotten logs, long histories of flesh, molecules like mine that have gone through many bodies and hurry to the ocean relieved. I was a human pushed into the water. I was a fish, a crab, a worm. I love how easy it is, to be alive. History does not break with a bang, but with a trickle. Victims define history. And in the river's throat, we all become equal. Where does blame belong, where does guilt lead us? When salt enters, the ocean accepts our final promise, to cease stating our point. Tomorrow's lost cultures. My body extinguished, its dark skin.

DEAD CHILD, REFRAMED

It's almost as if the child
was never real,
that child in the photograph,
skeletal,
his aged eyes
pointed to the left
of the photographer,
where his mother might be.
We can't see her body,
but there are flies on it,
and the buzz stops you as
the photographer winces,
replaces the lens cap.

Just outside the frame,
you imagine yourself that child
who could have lived.

ORNITHOLOGY

Father's fist still hurts from Sister's face.
This makes me weak like poison in the blood. The wind
invites me out. The grass is tender over broken glass
and excrement as rough practitioners of love touch under
the tree, let go. I too should let it go, if not
for her small face, small fire,
her black eye,
her fear of darkness.

She flies in her dreams.

She stutters, in her eyes a history of loss.
She expects pain, prepares for less than worst, thinks
in hopeless symbols, soars through fear and longing
all day and graduates to darkness in the evening.
At night, she listens to her future,
clear like birdsong.

There is no bird.

HOW THINGS FIT

Father in the well with his bright buttons. His eyes on my face above. His long beard like sand. My hands on the rope. My rope on his throat. He made it this way, you see. Sister's blue neck. Sheep in green hills of silence. It's been a long summer.

*

Mother's neck till she almost choked. Sister, she walked funny. The apple not ripe, but Father had to take. Water from the well washed away the blood. I bled too, remember. How can I forgive myself? Cherries, full of light. Grain thick with purpose.

*

Before Father, his father. Sister lies unblinking. Teeth on the pillow. Need to run, you see, but can't. Mother not breathing. Father laughs and takes another drink. I hide in the forest. Water lilies sing white. Bugs on the surface.

*

Got his buttons in fake war, a fake hero. Mother, Sister, gone. Father's vicious smirk, stink, drink, sweat. A path of bones has led us here. The child of a child with a broken face. Wind, a kind presence. Perfect dawns unnoticed.

*

Father by the well. A small push. Sister, Mother smile in my head. Father and his screams, his anger. My hands on the rope. Father in the well. Safe. His hands were blood. Water in the well cold, clear, like memory. Yellow, red eyes of apples. A pause between field and forest.

*

All blood that flowed, I bled too. I didn't die. How to forgive myself? Woods, green gaps of time. Tender haystacks full of shadow.

*

I'm in the well with Father. Stars stare down. Not long to wait. Father, already cold. Cold inside bone. Each life a promise, but we poison the water with our bodies.

BATTLEFIELD

This
skeleton
by the burning
cannon. I
take her hand. I
see her inner curves, now
transparent. I
love how more
than emptiness
remains. This
extinction. This
extermination. This
beautiful sand.

My
damaged muscle,
tendon, my
burned-out eyes, my
inward stare
without them. This
listening while
we still can. This
dark wood. This
blue sky, this
steep hill.

This
dead river. This
beautiful sand. This
lovely body I long for, this
vast world with many
dark hiding places
for those
like us, whose
bones lie lightly,
longing for symmetry.

THE ENDING

My father trains me in the art of death.
The red art.
He says,
> *There are too many of us to fit in the future.*
>> *We must be strong to survive.*
His bow is quick in his hands,
his arrow sharpened by determination.

A soft rustle,
and it's released,
> so eloquent in violence,
> unwilling to be still.
Its victim, my friend Ahmed, the dark-skinned boy, a slave.
The thump of the impact
> and he bends more than in half,
a red bloom
> in his heart,
>> a tall stem
>>> growing out of the flower.

I see a glint in Father's eyes,
> and in an instant I learn the threat of friendship:
>> the way we harm, not meaning to,
>>> the curse of being near.
I run to Ahmed;
> a hiss escapes his lips.

I smell the secrets of his opened body.

*

Did you see me stretch?
        Did you see me aim?
my father says,
        You have to feel it in your fingers.
            You must become one with death to take a life.
            You must love the wound.

*

I have practiced enough,
        but I don't want it to be known.
One night
        I will tie a note to my arrow
            and shoot it into Leila's window,
so we can set off on the road
and travel to a place
where my father's arrows
        can't reach us.

*

My son,
a shameless traitor.
I lost him years ago.
His will is weak,
        his heart unprepared for struggle.
His girl confessed.
One night,
when he makes a move,
my arrow will love him better than I can.

*

Red is a memory
       of things that haven't happened yet.
They wait
       just outside reach,
           stuck on time's axis.
Red thoughts visit late at night,
       when the future's whisper
           is within earshot.

I feel I could extend myself
       just so slightly—
and I'll know the whole story,
       know how it ends
           and what comes after.

But when morning comes,
       I forget once again.

I have to trust my skills,

let my story play itself through
to its unknown ending.

REFUGEE

It's not her face
that makes me think

of the past, but the way
she folds her hands, as if

each moment were a prayer,

a patient attendance to ritual. My hands
attempt to fold, but I

don't let them: I feel the weight
of being born too late

to be saved and too early

for immortality. My life will not be cast
in sky. The woman in the cell ignores

my doubts. My face is one
she hates by default, has every

right to in this forced

arrangement—the boil of history,
its violent interpretation, its tender

way of squeezing air out
of us one breath at

a time.

DRIVING LESSON

We go for a drive.

*

A woman steps from her hut,
her skin
time-tested like clay,

her thoughts clear like the river
four miles away
where she walks for water.

She leaves her children home.

*

The sudden sandstorm
like a whisper of hair
in the wind.

*

A child opens her eyes
into sand.

*

We leave the car
lights on.

We have to jump-start.

*

Light dies if you leave it alone.

*

The sand resembles water
in taste and memory.

*

The sun does not speak.

*

The woman sends her thoughts
back home
as sand envelops her lips.

*

We start the car in silence.

CONFRONTING THE BODY

What kind of silence boils in a heart
that's stopped? The shadow of a dead man's cheek
rests between my head and the pillow, keeps
its vigil. No one chronicles years
of absence. Don't call a house by its name. Elsewhere,
a market floor is slippery with fish. Here,
my face in the toilet; the interrogator
laughs like a muffled radio.

*

a line
and a line that
                              breaks
official postcard
                    a name
official words
unlawful combatant
a voice
                    in
the desert

a silence where
                    should be
a voice.

*

When heavy metal blasts my cell for days
I imagine a true guitar. Patient,
it awaits its turn to sing.

Do things sing?

No water
torture today. There is something
wrong with the guitar.

It has no strings.

*

God, I make my bed in you, your strong spine its frame, your lovely
      heart-shaped heart
            my pillow, your lies my safety
raft so I don't drown in my lack of substance, so I can make your beauti-
      ful, ruinous choices.

*

I'm not
not
myself
crack

between light and
light
white mouth
of truth
its lost eyes

bright teeth
I'm on boil

I'm not here
is not a choice
I can make
nothing sharp

bright
teeth
on the

floor

*

In this torture tool,
Palestinian Chair,
my hands chained
to an iron
ring in the floor,
my leg
muscles ache then hurt then
break.

Yes, it's true: some futures are
shorter than the rest.

Some

silences last longer than others.

*

A body opened along the wrong
seam gives the wrong
answer, becomes
its own obstacle.

A small skeleton with hands,
a heart and broken
words, a target,
a seam around
a knife.

*

Sun's grave is ours, dug for us—mystery
in sewn pockets, gold on our weakened
breath. Handcuffs. Diamonds in our eyes
where light should be. Interrogation philosophy.
This path, how was it made ours? Who
waged what inside us? There is always
more than we know: closed windows
in our minds, shadows shaped
from our hands, moss
on our lips.

ONTOLOGY

A bullet-size hole
in my chest; my best

attempts at love escape. A story
of wrong doors opened

in a wrong order. A multiple

choice test. A towel I left
on the beach

the morning
my mother ran out of air.

LIGHTENING

I wrap my mother's body in a small blanket. She is light in my arms. Sprawled by a fig tree, my father asks, *Are thoughts made of our own flesh?* I hesitate. *Our flesh is a ship stripped of sails.* We listen to the sound of the oars. A fig falls into my opening palm. *Bodies are evolving myths.* My mother is lighter and lighter each year.

ON FIRE, LOVE, KILLING, AND OTHER ITEMS

You, in the garden, among
growing things, in the far
corner, silent, more shadow
than person.

When I hand you a knife, I
don't mean *cut me open*.
I mean *feed me*. I
imagine a fire. You are welcome by it.

I'm lost in the dark
this side of
the door you closed behind
you. You are embedded in me.

When I say *bring
the firewood*, I
don't mean *burn me*.
I don't mean only *ash*. I also mean *love*.

Memory's not enough. When you said
remember me, I hope you meant *forget me*.

When I say *wait*, I mean *survive*,
be there.

UNFALLING THE STARS

sorry door
if I must bother you
why don't you open wider and admit friends

sorry song
my mouth is not fit to sing you

sorry distance
my steps are not wide enough to cover you

so many stars fall

last words hang over the threshold
in an endless conversation with my past
as I hang myself on a hat hook

in someone else's childhood
while you laugh like you always do

so many stars shine
sorry life

my words are not wide enough to honor you

BRIEF REDISCOVERY OF MINERALS

A distant bird, dissatisfied by darkness, says the first word.

Minerals lie until broken.

Bees remember their drone in lives before this one.

If a fish wants to be photographed, it finds a hook with a fly.

A bee is more beautiful because of the honey.

Birds tell me things they don't know but I do.

I remember being dead before the bees reminded me.

Minerals can wait for the final word.

OXYGEN

In many cases the oxygen in the air plays a part in the hardening process.
—PRIMO LEVI

OBITUARY

I envy air, its discreet noninvolvement
with our vision, except to paint the sky

a fake blue, or to serve as a canvas

for dawn. I wish I could summon myself
invisibly like the wind. I wish I could be

cleared. What wouldn't I give for a little

transparency. Even polluted, I will not
complain. Even cancer is part of me. In the end,

I will be smoke over your city. I envy

the spaces between things.

BRIEF INTERVIEW WITH THE DEAD

I asked the dead
isn't every day a tuning fork
for the next?
isn't each of us a rehearsal
for others?

and they replied
don't worry
it need not make sense
your death
is less than a lifetime away

UNARCHAEOLOGY

I'm trying to reach a small city hidden by the sand dunes. Sand, are you one or many? City, are you made of sand? Dusty hut, only one window is open, and on the floor, a smaller dune blown in by the wind. You still breathe, sand on your tongue, your white robes gray from sand. In the basket resting in the doorframe's shadow hides the diamond. My eyes burn from the sand. The knife, the hand, imprinted in memory. I should not have been here. In the bag of sandy shadows, an empty flask. A path outside, red dawn. Diamond, was it worth it? Sand, what's your last wish?

APERTURES

These are the days when nothing
stays long in our blood. Our hopes

are red rivers that run
into the heart
and die there.

Forgive me if I
wave even if you're gone. In
our bodies

more is hidden than found. What light
defines this afternoon over the fields

and your eyes?
Tree rings; crow
feet. Red

rivers' ending. Inside
and outside, vast
distances lie,

unexplored; a single life. The period
after this sentence is

a land mine.

BATTLEFIELD

A boy dies, a girl bleeds.
A stranger brings a head on a plate.
You forget your keys.
Every time, love turns to dust in your hands.
Reason hangs loose on a thread of logic.
Harmony calls, so close you can feel
its sharp edge in yourself.
Locked in us, years melt. Eyes
close every time they open.

ON FIRE, LOVE, KILLING, AND OTHER ITEMS

A seed grows into a house, a thought
into a forest. Some of us carry centuries on
our backs, some branches of fruit. Some carry
nothing. In the corner, a key is hidden in a child's heart,
and the cipher is lost. The way by the river is also the way
by your cemetery. Silence burns at both ends. The house grows
into memory. The child grows into an apple tree. I'm beginning to taste

its thoughts.

THE OTHER KINDNESS

I reach inside a deer
to extract a life

to touch directly
is the simplest kindness

like being the other

like the gift of knowing in advance
or expecting the same in return

like a loving hand inside me
stopping my heart

*

I open the angle
of the bird's flight
become a wing torn off

the calendar like a deer
that lived long ago
in this world

or in one of our stories
or a tree not yet

firm as a tree
like a small truth
smaller than I

may have thought
smaller than the footprint
of my years

*

who is the other
who opens the door
whose words change me
whose shadow makes my shadow

lighter

like the gift of never
knowing one day
there will be no distance
between me and my body

no difference

between my age
and the length of my life
the calendar
shreds its wings

yet the bird flies

the deer runs
like putting my hand
inside myself
in an act of kindness

already blind and waiting

for the future to swallow the rest
like reaching into myself
already not quite myself
knowing what

I am about to find

BLUEPRINTS FOR REBUILDING

All doors are open
to the future, all dictionaries
replaced, the windows turned
around to face our origins. Should
we look?
Tight bundles of reasons move
below the surface of our lives. We reject past
choices, yet we think of ourselves
continuing. Are you a rock thrown
into the river, or a cloud on its rush

to rain?

Let's watch the animals
watch us. In the kitchen, fake
fruits wait, trapped in permanence.
Open the window. Each
awkward star shines, bored to death.
Which *you* do I know? Which *I*
would I be if our stories hadn't crossed?
Do you wonder about the body
giving up its skills one
by one? I remember: when invited, damage
stays. The house unfolds, a slow
flower with new dictionaries, grass
under the coffee table, moss wallpaper.
Let me see it through
your impossible eyes.

Will I

recognize you among
the many animals, so perfect in their shape,
their run, their warm fur, their bright
teeth? In the garden, plastic flowers
linger. Are you a rock or a
cloud? Tell me about giving up
in a good way. What
if the foundation happens
last? What
name should
I answer to?

HANDFULNESS

One hand for danger, one
for smoothing the tired brow. Crow

feet in my eyes, crow nests
in my apple tree, spider

webs for blossoms, their blind
shimmer. How did time turn

into responsibility? Or was it
the lack of time, the brevity

of each blood cell, each
busy century? My blood is

too old to sing—it can only
whisper. In each crow nest, a stolen

nightingale egg. The cracked
hymn of dying. I still

hold out a piece of bread in one
hand.

STILLED LIFE

You raise
your hand,
and the moment

stops,

broken up along
        its   axis. Calm

                                     where fear used to be
    and a new

electricity coursing through veins.

You are
        a drowned
                          star with a rock
in each pocket. Between
                    us,
everything
           weighed in time,
                    blood and breath.

*

You stop
          the car in
the middle of silence,

                  and time burns.

This is all
we have

to offer—   thoughts

in the wind

and a flame.

*

May the car
            keep
                        running and take us
to our un-

                                    predictable future
            where
fire   consumes

everything but the bone, then

                        eats away the bone—after
all,

the dead have
            no use for it. Sometimes
                        broken

things

                        matter.

*

I've tried all

sorts of silences to say
something small, smaller
than one can hear.

PLANNING FOR MY LIFE

This life I so strangely inhabit:
why me?
The stones,

the rain.
Out of billions of possibilities,
how did I come along?

May my life be a crossed reference
for how to make the best and the worst
of what is

and is not,

for speaking to stones
in their ageless whisper,
for talking to rain

in its intricate touch.
Some think of memory
in terms of forgetting.

If blood was spilled,
why not say it was mine?
If anything remains,

may this remain:

the best blueprint
necessary
to rebuild

the possibility of me,
the chance of you,
the life we so strangely inhabit,

the centuries,
the smile,
the rain,

the stones.

OBITUARY

I take no issue with glass.
It loves well.
It opens views, veins,
is cut with a diamond. I'm sorry,
but I like its reflective
nature, its depth, its
transparency.
I love its crunch
on my teeth. I value how
it pushes against
the wind.
It doesn't mean
to be in the bird's
path. What goes
through the bird's mind? Mine
dissects the bird, finds
its lost
symmetry, forgives
its broken wings.
I'm sorry, but this
is the only life
I have. I think of all
the water I
can pour into it.
I take no issue
with blood, salty like
the sea. And dreams,
bridges into truth.

I'm sorry, but I failed
to love the way love should
be done, and I'll fail
again. When stillness
takes hold, you will
remain. I'll hide
among reflections
glass remembers.
I take no issue with
missing things.

INNER METEOROLOGY

I'm in favor of wind,

its passage, time's passage
(here, insert everything

whose passage affects you).
We all can use a small

break. I try to light myself on fire,

sing like the wind, like
the wolf, but my vocal range

is a poor match. In my heart,
the wind swirls no matter what.

I'm winded like a toy, but I try

not to be dull. The wolf
mocks me. Maybe the wind will

knock down some trees. We all
can use a small blackout,

a windy dark night. In the midst

of transparency air
plans its assault. We blow it again,

wind's orphans. The wolf
hides in my heart.

ENTRAPMENT

Why does the sky curve in this light? The fallen leaves do a better job of remembering. I drop my glove into the water. Mist lingers. Two gaunt men with absent faces carry a child's body, the river's offering. It's someone's fault, perhaps mine. The owl's cry echoes in the distance. Am I the child? Just because I stopped to look at the sky, do I have to be in this story?

UNKNOWLEDGE

I don't understand why
the ground is where things fall to.

I wonder why the wind labors
in random directions

and how a clock
remembers what year it is.

I marvel at the way a pen bleeds.
I don't understand what it takes

to be understood,
or how paper lies, flat, pale, unused.

I don't understand why
a life is longer than its parts

but shorter than a love letter.

PLANNING FOR MY LIFE

We had forgotten something,
and then it disappeared.

The sun's a crime,
horizon melting,
our lives misshapen by neglect.

But if our song should lose its path,
may myriads of buzzing seconds
envelop us, demanding harmony.

May nascent futures spin
and crash like cymbals
in our minds, unseen by others.

We know how it works. The sun dies
when not in use:
lonely, melting under a lid of night.

We must deliver,
if only to ourselves, we must shine.
We must belong in our lives.

When I'm born, remind me
to start again.

EXCESS OF LIGHT

I approve of the dark, its sharp corners, its long
branches, its imagined holes in the floor,

its disturbed strangers, its secrets that pretend to be

visible during the day. For the sake of beauty,
I'm in favor of less vs. more, zero vs.

one, a sad vs. happy ending in art, but not

life. For the sake of life, I befriend
strangers made from similar thoughts. Soon

it's my turn to be measured. My fading

eyes attest only to time's passing, not
the way I've used its passage. I fall

from my own hands. I'm a zero, a dark

corner. For the sake of truth,
I count myself among the secrets.

BRIEF REDISCOVERY OF MINERALS

If you believe in chemistry, you've learned: brief beings
with golden thoughts arise from minerals.

I'm something from before, something you said in passing.
I don't know you like this, in your own after.

The street corner looks the same, but I'm not here.
A green house, a blue house, a gray, a yellow. Our reliable memories.

Our impossible futures. I connect to you in thought.
Mine, then. Yours, now. I took a shorter path.

In some universe, we both exist. In some light,
we cast more than one shadow. You carry me back.

If you believe in alchemy, gold might fall into place
from simple elements on hand.

LOVE LETTER TO EVERYONE

We wait in line to become obsolete,
to trade places with shadows.

I turn around, and in the line behind me,
I see you, your face immense, intent
as only you can be.

If some of us are like you,
then all at once I'm less obsolete.

FUTURE HISTORY

If the right
      star
is lit, we will be
      the other side
of fire, its bright
      promise. The fire
will burn
our skins and darker
things in us.
      In the end,
there will be some
fire to keep.

PROPER DARKNESS

A railroad in winter.
A numb sky.
I hold my breath.
Even the most insignificant statements are final.
Words outlive silence.

What's uttered remains on both ends.

If only I could hide myself
under last year's mask of leaves,
absorb their colors.
Nothing we say amounts to what we mean,
yet we say.

I love the darkness in my mouth when it's closed.

NOTES

Primo Levi quotes are from *The Periodic Table*, translated by Raymond Rosenthal.

The epigraph by Dan Pagis is from *The Selected Poetry of Dan Pagis*, translated by Stephen Mitchell.

The last line in "Excess of Light" is a nod to Paul Celan.

"Ornithology" was inspired by a line from John Sibley Williams.

"The Ending": with gratitude to Paulann Petersen for her workshop springboards.

"Love Letter to Everyone" was originally presented as part of the *I See You* ekphrastic art project organized by *Elohi Gadugi Journal* and Artists' Milepost, Portland, Oregon.

ACKNOWLEDGMENTS

I am indebted to the editors of the following magazines and presses for publishing the following poems, in some cases under different titles:

Allbook Books: haiku excerpts from "Confronting the Body" and other poems.
Bennington Review: "The Tilt"
Cider Press Review: "Lightening," "Ornithology"
The Cincinnati Review: "Obituary" (2)
concīs: "Ontology"
Contrary: "The Ending"
Fixional: "Brief Rediscovery of Minerals" (1) and (2), "Unarchaeology," "Battlefield" (3)
Ghost Town Poetry and *The Oregonian*: "Broken Borders"
Hawai'i Review: "Pontist's Dream"
Identity Theory: "Late to the World"
Indianapolis Review: "How Things Fit," "Handfulness"
Mad Hatters' Review: "Planning for My Life," "Violin Lesson"
New Orleans Review: "Unchronology," "Driving Lesson" (2)
Pif: "Driving Lesson" (1)
The Pinch: "Unfinality"
Poetry Northwest: "Proper Darkness"
Ruminate: "Unhistory"
Seneca Review: "Apertures"
Sequestrum: "Excess of Light," "A Bright Pile of Reasons," "Key"
Spillway: excerpt from "Confronting the Body"
Tampa Review: "Since all your friends"

Toe Good Poetry: "Battlefield" (2)

Volt: "The Other Kindness," "On Fire, Love, Killing, and Other Items" (1),
    "Moon in the River"

"Opened," "Broken Borders," "Metal, Deciphered," "Correction," "Unfalling
the Stars," and "Late to the World" were published by Toe Good Poetry in
The Invention of Distance, a chapbook.

Thanks to Elizabeth J. Colen for her review of the manuscript.

My most sincere gratitude to the members of The Moonlit Poetry Caravan
and The Odds for their help with revisions:

Frances Payne Adler, Jon Backman, Dale Baker, Devon Balwit, Judith
Barrington, Aron Bernstein, Jon Boisvert, Erica Braverman, Meghan
Caughey, April Curfman, Brenna Dimmig, Gerry Foote, Kathy French, Diane Holland, Juleen Johnson, Josh Keen, Mike Langtry, Janis Lull, James
Maynard, John Morrison, Emily Newberry, Paulann Petersen, Katharine
Quince, Willa Schneberg, Sam Seskin, Joseph Soldati, Dianne Stepp, Mark
Struzan, Jeff Whitney, John Sibley Williams.

I'm especially grateful to my editor, Danielle Cadena Deulen, for her insightful suggestions that have made the work so much better. And thanks to
Nicola Mason, Lisa Ampleman, and everyone else at Acre Books for making
this book happen.

Special thanks to Laurie for being there.